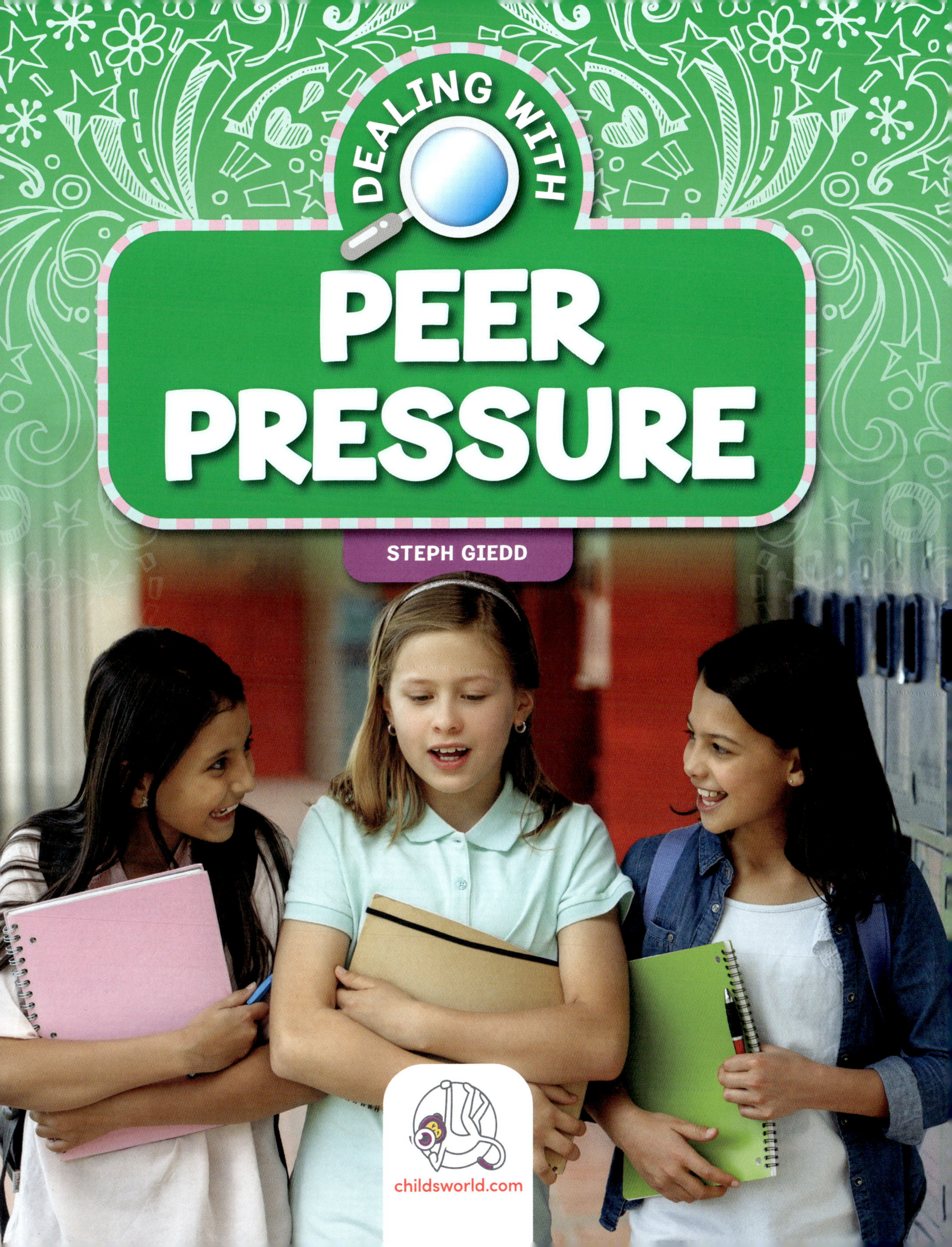
DEALING WITH
PEER PRESSURE
STEPH GIEDD
childsworld.com

Published by The Child's World®
800-599-READ • www.childsworld.com

Photography Credits
Photographs ©: iStockphoto, cover, 1, 10–11, 14; Shutterstock Images, 5, 6 (top), 6 (middle), 6 (bottom), 12–13, 18–19; Robert Kneschke/Shutterstock Images, 9; Monkey Business Images/Shutterstock Images, 16–17; Fam Veld/Shutterstock Images, 20; Highwaystarz Photography/iStockphoto, 22

ISBN Information
9781503885363 (Reinforced Library Binding)
9781503885622 (Portable Document Format)
9781503886261 (Online Multi-user eBook)
9781503886902 (Electronic Publication)

LCCN 2023937513

Printed in the United States of America

Steph Giedd is a former high school English teacher who now works as an editor. Originally from southern Iowa, Giedd lives in Minneapolis, Minnesota, with her husband, daughter, and pets.

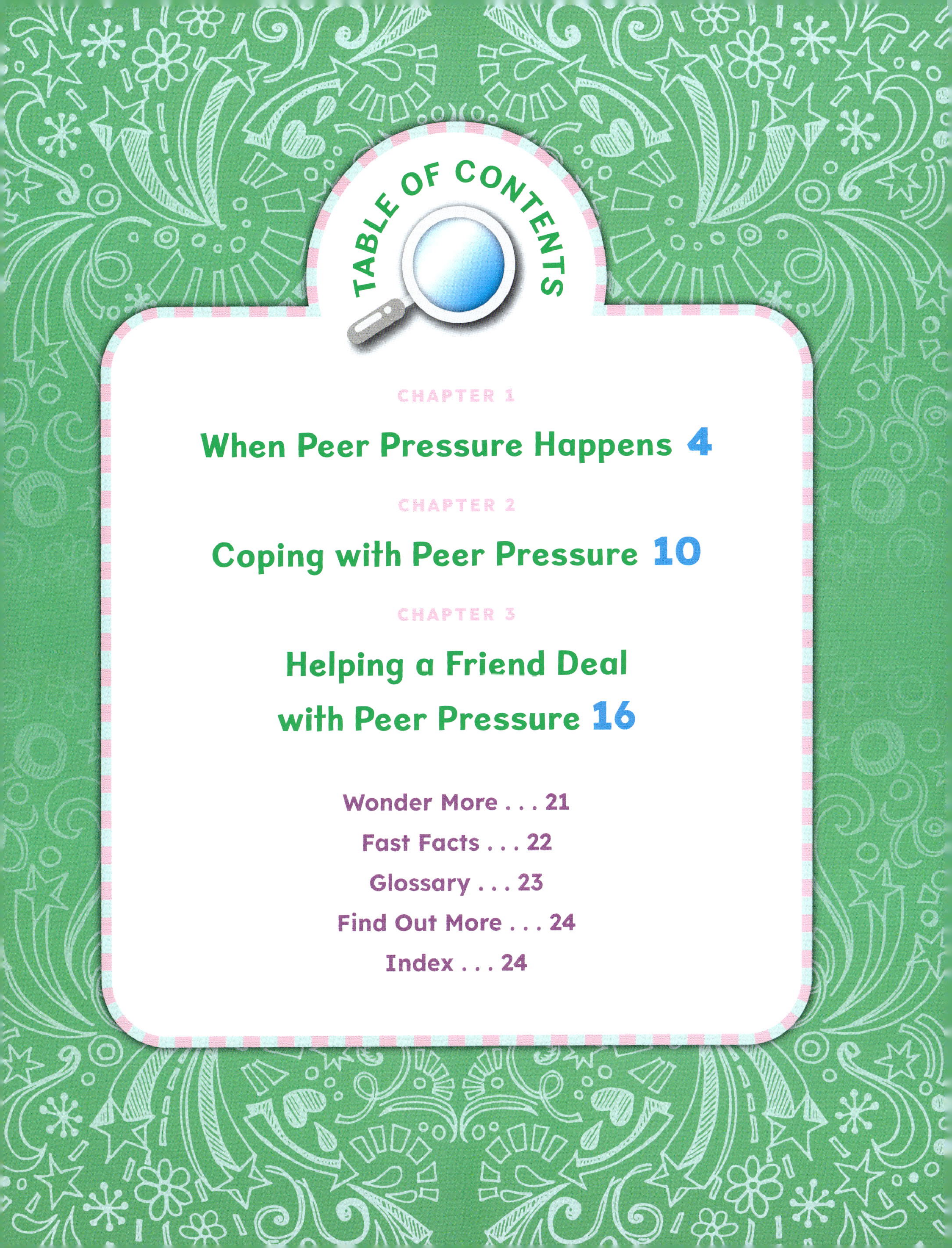

TABLE OF CONTENTS

When Peer Pressure Happens

Sometimes people feel pressure from others to act, dress, talk, or think a certain way. This is called peer pressure. Peers are people or friends who are close in age. They may be interested in similar things.

Sometimes peers push a person to do something he or she may not want to do. That is negative peer pressure. When peers push each other to act or think a certain way, it can make a person feel **conflicted** and upset.

School is one place where peer pressure can happen.

What to Say Instead

It can be easy to say things that might pressure someone, even without meaning to. People can be accepting of differences to avoid pressuring their peers. People can also focus on making choices for themselves instead of for others.

Pressuring Speech	Accepting Speech
"I hate spaghetti. You should get pizza instead."	"I'm going to get pizza. I hope you like the spaghetti!"
"Football is boring. No one plays football anymore."	"I like soccer more than football. If we play football today, can we play soccer tomorrow?"
"Wearing mittens isn't cool. You should put on gloves instead."	"I'm not a big fan of mittens, but you should wear whatever you like best."

People might not know what to do when they are pressured. If people don't give in to pressure, their peers might make them feel as if they don't fit in. They may feel **excluded**.

For example, a person might be pressured to buy and wear expensive new shoes that everyone else has. But he may not actually like the shoes. He might feel he needs to get them just to fit in. And if the shoes are expensive, he may feel conflicted about asking his parents to buy them. But if he doesn't get the shoes, he might worry that people are judging him.

Peers might also pressure their friends to break the rules. This negative peer pressure could lead to doing something unsafe. It's important for people to **resist** negative peer pressure. They should always do what they believe is right.

People can experience positive peer pressure, too. It can be good to **encourage** a peer to be confident, brave, or a better friend. This could mean helping someone overcome a fear, such as talking in front of a big group. People can learn how to encourage their friends in positive ways.

People can encourage their friends by celebrating when they succeed.

Coping with Peer Pressure

If a person feels pressured to act or think in a certain way, she should take a moment to think about her feelings. A person shouldn't do something just because she thinks everybody else is doing it. People's **instincts** are usually correct when they feel that something is wrong. People should listen to their gut response.

A person can step away to think about his feelings before giving in to peer pressure.

It is important for people to think about what is right and safe. When deciding if something is safe, a person might ask himself if the action could hurt someone. Is it kind to everyone involved? Does it exclude anyone? Is it allowed? If something is against the rules, there is probably a good reason why. Understanding the rules can help people do the right thing.

There are many ways to handle peer pressure. First, people can simply say no to whatever they are being pressured to do. They can walk away from whomever is pressuring them. Walking away shows they won't give in to the pressure. If the pressure doesn't stop, they can get help from an adult.

Walking away from negative peer pressure can be hard.

People can talk to their parents about excuses they might use in pressure situations.

Plan Ahead!

Being pressured by a peer can feel overwhelming. People can plan ahead so they know what to say in those situations. A person could practice saying, "I don't feel safe doing that." He or she could also try saying, "I don't want to get in trouble. I'm not going to break the rules."

People who are being pressured can also make up an excuse not to give in to the pressure. This can help someone get out of a pressure situation. They might say their parents won't let them do something. Many parents are comfortable being used as an excuse.

People can avoid peer pressure by spending time with people who are supportive. Good friends will speak up for others. They will support people making their own choices. It's OK not to fit in with every group. It's OK not to follow every new **trend**.

Helping a Friend Deal with Peer Pressure

People can help friends who are dealing with peer pressure. First, they can be a positive example for their friends. They can do the right and safe thing all the time. Others will follow that example.

When a friend is feeling pressured, people can help the friend stand up to the person pressuring him. People can also help their friend walk away from the situation. Afterward, people can listen to how their friend is feeling. Together, they can make a plan for what to do if the friend is pressured again.

Good friends won't exclude people for not giving in to peer pressure.

Friends can help each other stay safe on the playground.

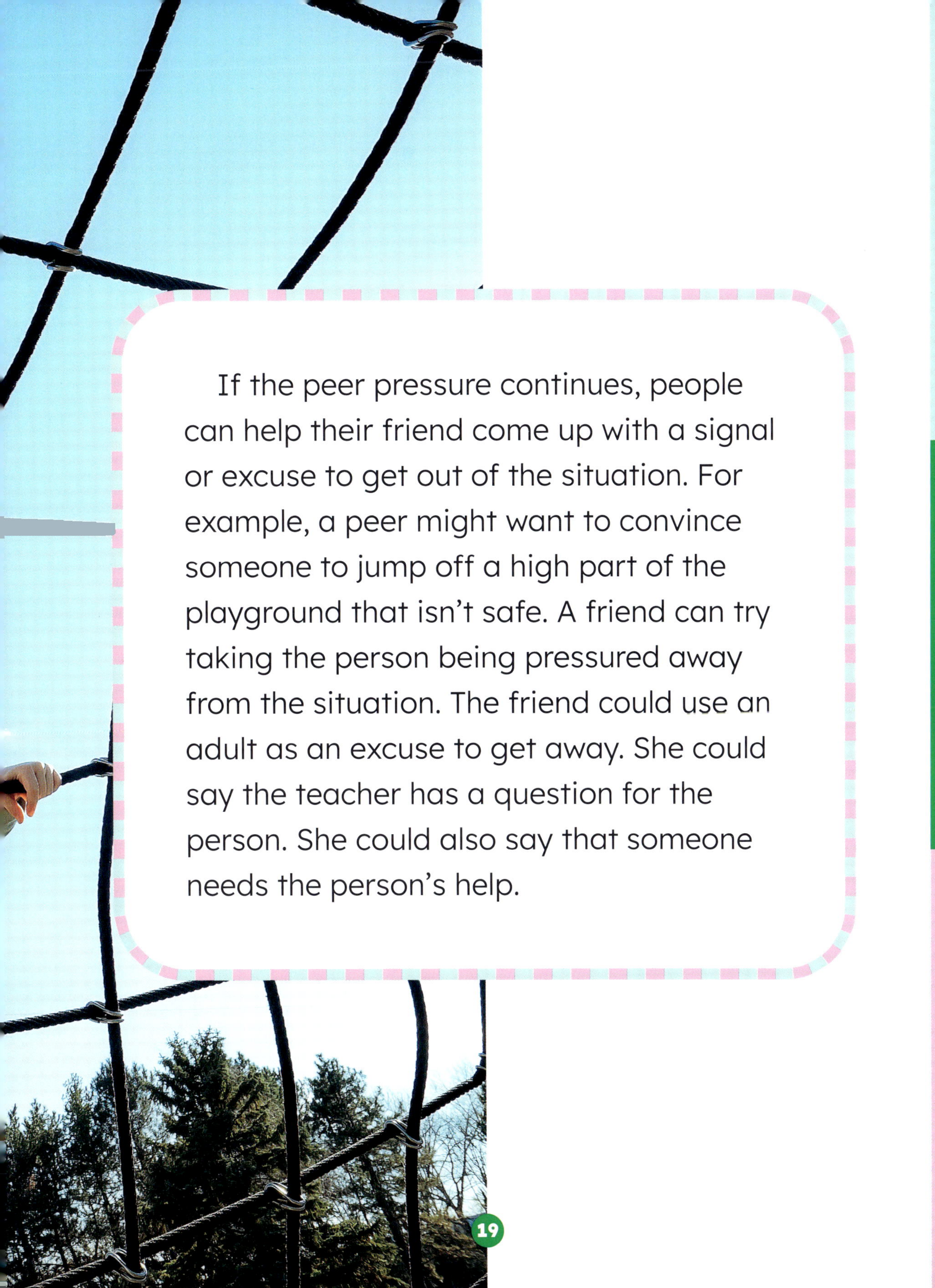

If the peer pressure continues, people can help their friend come up with a signal or excuse to get out of the situation. For example, a peer might want to convince someone to jump off a high part of the playground that isn't safe. A friend can try taking the person being pressured away from the situation. The friend could use an adult as an excuse to get away. She could say the teacher has a question for the person. She could also say that someone needs the person's help.

Doing something new can be easier with a friend.

If the pressure is positive, a person could ask his friend to try something new when she is ready. It can be hard to try new things. But he can encourage his friend to be brave.

Peer pressure can be hard to handle. But good friends will respect one another's choices. It is important for all people to be themselves.

Wonder More

Wondering about New Information

How much did you know about peer pressure before reading this book? What new information did you learn? Write down three new facts that this book taught you. Was the new information surprising? Why or why not?

Wondering How It Matters

What is one way peer pressure relates to your life? If you cannot think of a personal connection, imagine how the topic might affect other kids. What impact might it have on their lives?

Wondering Why

Why might peer pressure be positive? Describe an example of positive peer pressure.

Ways to Keep Wondering

Peer pressure is an important topic to learn about. After reading this book, what questions do you have about it? What can you do to learn more about dealing with peer pressure?

Fast Facts

- Peers are friends or people of the same age who may like similar things.
- Peer pressure can be positive or negative.
- Negative peer pressure can make people do things that are not right or safe.
- It is OK for people to walk away from pressure situations. They can practice what to do in these situations before they happen. That way, they will be prepared.
- To help a friend deal with negative peer pressure, someone can help the person come up with a reason to leave the pressure situation.
- People can talk to an adult about peer pressure and what to do in those situations.
- Someone who feels pressured can spend time with people who do the right and safe things.

Glossary

conflicted (kon-FLIK-ted) Someone who isn't sure what to do or think feels conflicted. A student felt conflicted when pressured to do something that he didn't think was safe.

encourage (en-KUR-ej) To encourage someone means to give him or her support and confidence. When people encourage their friends to try something new, that is positive peer pressure.

excluded (ex-KLOO-duhd) Being excluded means that someone is left out of a group or activity. If someone is judged for not giving in to peer pressure, she might feel excluded.

instincts (IN-stinktz) Instincts are people's first reactions to something. The friend's instincts were to follow the rules.

resist (ree-ZIST) To resist means to not do something even when being pressured to do it. People can resist peer pressure by making a plan for what to do in that situation.

trend (TREND) A trend is something that is popular, usually for a short amount of time. People might pressure others to follow a new trend.

Find Out More

In the Library

An, Priscilla. *Mindfulness with Friends.* Parker, CO: The Child's World, 2024.

Golkar, Golriz. *Facing Peer Pressure.* Minneapolis, MN: Jump, 2023.

Kelly, Sheila M., and Shelly Rotner. *All Kinds of Friends.* Minneapolis, MN: Lerner, 2018.

On the Web

Visit our website for links about dealing with peer pressure:

childsworld.com/links

Note to Parents, Caregivers, Teachers, and Librarians: We routinely verify our Web links to make sure they are safe and active sites. So encourage your readers to check them out!

Index